First World War
and Army of Occupation
War Diary
France, Belgium and Germany

61 DIVISION
Divisional Troops
61 Sanitary Section
24 May 1916 - 30 April 1917

WO95/3052/1

The Naval & Military Press Ltd
www.nmarchive.com
Published in association with The National Archives

Published by

The Naval & Military Press Ltd

Unit 10 Ridgewood Industrial Park,

Uckfield, East Sussex,

TN22 5QE England

Tel: +44 (0) 1825 749494

www.naval-military-press.com

www.nmarchive.com

This diary has been reprinted in facsimile from the original. Any imperfections are inevitably reproduced and the quality may fall short of modern type and cartographic standards.

© Crown Copyright
Images reproduced by permission of The National Archives, London, England, 2015.

Contents

Document type	Place/Title	Date From	Date To
Heading	WO95/3052/1		
Heading	61st Division 61 Sanitary Section 1916 May-1917 Apl To 4 Army		
Heading	61st Divisional Sanitary Section May 1916		
War Diary	Cholderton	24/05/1916	24/05/1916
War Diary	Southampton	24/05/1916	24/05/1916
War Diary	Le Havre	26/05/1916	27/05/1916
War Diary	Merville	28/05/1916	28/05/1916
War Diary	St Venant	31/05/1916	31/05/1916
Heading	61st Divn Sany Sector June 1916		
War Diary	St Venant	01/06/1916	10/06/1916
War Diary	Le Gorgue	11/06/1916	28/06/1916
Heading	War Diary of 61st Div Sanitary Section 61st Division July 1916 Vol 3		
War Diary	La Gorgue	01/07/1916	31/07/1916
Heading	War Diary of 61st Div Sanitary Section From 1st August To 31st August 1916 Vol 4		
War Diary	La Gorgue	01/08/1916	31/08/1916
Heading	War Diary of 61st Divisional Sanitary Section From 1st Sept 1916 To 30th Sept 1916 Volume 5		
War Diary	La Gorgue	01/09/1916	30/09/1916
Heading	War Diary 61st Divisional Sanitary Section From Oct 1st To Oct 31st 1916 Volume 6		
War Diary	La Gorgue	01/10/1916	27/10/1916
War Diary	St Venant	28/10/1916	31/10/1916
Heading	War Diary of 61st Div Sanitary Section From 1st Nov 16 To 30th Nov 16 Volume No.7		
War Diary	St Venant	01/11/1916	01/11/1916
War Diary	Chelers	02/11/1916	03/11/1916
War Diary	Rollecourt	04/11/1916	05/11/1916
War Diary	Frohen Le Grand	06/11/1916	14/11/1916
War Diary	Bernaville	15/11/1916	15/11/1916
War Diary	Canaples	16/11/1916	16/11/1916
War Diary	Contay	17/11/1916	21/11/1916
War Diary	W.7.b.4.27 Sheet 57d S	22/11/1916	30/11/1916
Heading	War Diary of 61st Divisional Sanitary Section From 1st December 16 To 31st December 16 Volume No.8		
War Diary	W.7.b.7.2 Sheet 57.d.s	01/12/1916	31/12/1916
Heading	War Diary of 61st Div Sanitary Section From 1/2/17 To 28/2/17 Volume No.10		
War Diary	W7.b.7.2 Sheet 57d	01/02/1917	05/02/1917
War Diary	Long	06/02/1917	13/02/1917
War Diary	Guillaucourt	14/02/1917	17/02/1917
War Diary	Harbonniers	18/02/1917	28/02/1917
Heading	War Diary of 61st Div Sanitary Section From 1st March 1917 To 31st March 1917 Volume Number 11		
War Diary	Harbonnieres	01/03/1917	28/03/1917
War Diary	Croix Molignaux	29/03/1917	31/03/1917
Heading	War Diary of 61st Div Sanitary Section For April 1917 Volume No.12		

| War Diary | Croix Molignaux D 849 Sheet 62c | 01/04/1917 | 10/04/1917 |
| War Diary | Croix Molignaux | 11/04/1917 | 30/04/1917 |

130 95 / 30 52 / 1

61ST DIVISION

61 ~~DIVL~~ SANITARY SECTION
~~MAY–DEC 1916~~
1916 MAY — 1917 APL

To 4 ARMY

61st Divisional Sanitary Section

May 1916

WAR DIARY
or
INTELLIGENCE SUMMARY.
(Erase heading not required.)

Army Form C. 2118.

Opened on 24/5/16
by Lt H Davidson Capt RAMC
o/c 61 Sc Div Sanitary Section

Place	Date	Hour	Summary of Events and Information	Remarks and references to Appendices
Cheddar	29/5/16	1 PM	Unit left Cheddar for entrainment from Axbridge on S.S. "INVENTOR" for "LE HAVRE"	R 1
Southampton	"	7.30 PM	Embarked on S.S. "INVENTOR" for "LE HAVRE"	
Le Havre	30/5/16	4 AM	Arrived "LE HAVRE", disembarked and proceeded to No 1 REST CAMP	
Le Havre	31/5/16	3.30 PM	Entrained at Point H. LE HAVRE for Concentration Area	
Merville	1/6/16	6 AM	Detrained at MERVILLE, and marched to ST VENANT	
St Venant	3/5/16		Opened BATHING STATION at ST VENANT for bathing of 600 men daily	

Lt H Davidson Capt RAMC
o/c 61 Sc Div Sanitary Section

Col Dick Savoy Lecture

June 1946

61st (8th MIDD) DIV. SANITARY SEC:

Sanitary Sec: Vol 2

WAR DIARY or INTELLIGENCE SUMMARY.

Army Form C. 2118.

Place	Date	Hour	Summary of Events and Information	Remarks and references to Appendices
St Venant	1/10/16		Kitchen & Oven constructed for Div HQ for Sanitary Section	
"	2/10/16		" " "	
"	5/10/16		Div Laundry started	
"	9/10/16		Closed down Div Laundry and returned Clothing in Stock to X1d Corps Laundry	
"	10/10/16		O/c proceeded to 36th Div Area to take over from 179th Sanitary Section, with advance party of 4 N.C.O's	
La Gorgue	11/10/16		Div Baths taken over. Div Laundry at Pont du Hem, Pont Riquel & La Vente and Div Baths at St Venant closed down	
"	13/10/16		Unit moved from ST VENANT to LA GORGUE and Div Laundry & Baths at LA GORGUE taken over	
"	13/6/16		Water Supply & Wire taken over, and inspection of Water Carts in the Division commenced	
"	14/10/16		Sanitation of town of LAVENTE taken charge of by NCO of Sanitary Sect	
"	15/10/16		Inspection of Camps in LA GORGUE	
"	16/10/16		Inspection of huts in LA GORGUE	
"	19/10/16		Census of all Wells in LA GORGUE commenced	

Army Form C. 2118.

61st (2ND MID:) DIV. SANITARY SEC:

Instructions regarding War Diaries and Intelligence Summaries are contained in F. S. Regs., Part II. and the Staff Manual respectively. Title pages will be prepared in manuscript.

WAR DIARY
or
INTELLIGENCE SUMMARY.
(Erase heading not required.)

Place	Date	Hour	Summary of Events and Information	Remarks and references to Appendices
La Gorgue	27/9/16		Water Supply at LA GORGUE centre discontinued	
"	28/9/16		Water Supply centre at ESTAIRES taken over by Sanitary Section	
"	29/9/16		Census of old wells in LA GORGUE completed	
"	24/9/16		Water Supply centre restarted at LA GORGUE	
"	25/9/16		Census of wells in Divisional Area commenced	

M Dawson Capt RAMC
O/C 61st Div Sanitary Section

Vol. 3
of

Confidential

July 1916 War Diary of 101st Div. Sanitary Section
101st Division
Vol 3

July 1916

WAR DIARY or INTELLIGENCE SUMMARY.

Army Form C. 2118.

Place	Date	Hour	Summary of Events and Information	Remarks and references to Appendices
LA GORGUE	1/7/16		Inspection of Billets at LAVENTE Map reference M.14 & 5. Sheet 36 SW edition 7-A	(SM(1)
LA GORGUE	2/7/16		Inspection of Camps in LA GORGUE L.35 sheet 36A edition 6	(SM1)
"	3/7/16		Inspection of Billets in LA GORGUE L.35 " " "	(M1)
"	4/7/16		Inspection of Billets in LA GORGUE L.35 " " "	(SM1)
"	5/7/16		Improved Sanitary arrangements in LA GORGUE L.35 " " "	(M1)
"	6/7/16		Inspected Water Carts at Pumping Station L.34 & 6.W. Constructed Latrines at L.35 b 2.3	(SM1)
"	7/7/16		Constructed Cooking Kitchen and Meat Safe at L.35 b 2.3, Sheet 36A Edition 6	(SM2)
"	8/7/16		Inspection of Water Wells in LA GORGUE L.35. Sheet 36A Edition 6	(SM1)
LA GORGUE	9/7/16		Inspection of Water Wells in LAVENTE M.14 & 5. Sheet 36 SW Edition 7A	(SM1)
"	10/7/16		Improved Sanitary arrangements provided for Camps & Billets at LAVENTE M.14 & 5 sheet 36 SW Edition 7A	(SM1)
"	11/7/16		Inspection of Water Supplies in FORWARD AREA	(SM1)
LA GORGUE	12/7/16		Testing Samples of Water from FORWARD AREA	(SM1)
"	13/7/16		Tested further Water Samples from FORWARD AREA and LAVENTE	(SM1)
"	14/7/16		Construction Sanitation carried out for various units	(SM1)
LA GORGUE	15/7/16		Meat Inspection & food at Salvage Stores, LA GORGUE L.34 D.1.4 Sheet 36A Edition 6	(SM1)

Army Form C. 2118.

WAR DIARY
or
INTELLIGENCE SUMMARY.
(Erase heading not required.)

Place	Date	Hour	Summary of Events and Information	Remarks and references to Appendices
LA GORGUE	16/11/16		Chlorinating Sedimentation apparatus fixed at PICANTIN POST M.6 & 6.2 Sheet 36 SW Edition 7A	SAD
"	17/11/16		O.C. proceeded to RED HOUSE to assist with wounded M.6.d.2.1. "	6 APD
"	18/11/16		"	4 APD
LA GORGUE	18/11/16		Inspection of Camps in LA GORGUE L.35 Sheet 36a Edition 6	4 APD
"	19/11/16		Inspection of Billets in LA GORGUE L.35 "	5 APD
LA GORGUE	20/11/16		Inspection of Camps in LAVENTE M.4 & 5 Sheet 36 SW Edition 7A	6 APD
"	21/11/16		Inspection of Sanitary arrangements of Billets in LAVENTE Sheet 36 SW Edition 7A	5 APD
"	22/11/16		Water Census of Divisional AREA Completed	6 APD
"	23/11/16		Relabelling of all Wells in Divisional Area Commenced.	6 APD
LA GORGUE	24/11/16		Carting Sheet refuse in LA GORGUE Commenced L.35 Sheet 36a Edition 6	5 APD
"	25/11/16		Rotary Sanitary arrangements provided for 24 Marseilles L.34 & L.4 Sheet 36a Edition 6	5 APD
"	26/11/16		Inspection of Billets at Rothead L.35 & 2 Sheet 36a Edition 6	5 APD
"	"		Inspection of Sanitary arrangements in FORWARD AREA	6 APD
"	27/11/16		Inspection of Water Carts in DIVISIONAL AREA	6 APD
"	28/11/16		General Sanitation in LA GORGUE L.35 Sheet 36a Edition 6	6 APD
"	29/11/16		Inspected food at Salvage Stores of 162 Bde & inspection of Billets LAVENTE M.4 & 5 Sheet 36 SW Edition 7A	6 APD
"	30/11/16		Inspected Preserved Meat at Railhead LA GORGUE L.35 b.2. Sheet 36a Edition 6	6 APD
"	30/11/16		Inspected meat at Railhead L.35.B.2 & Inspection of Water Carts at L.34.C.6.4 Sheet 36a Edition 6	5 APD

W. H. Dawson
Capt RAMC
O/C 1st W Div Sanitary Section

Confidential

Vol 4

WAR DIARY
of 61st Div Sanitary Section

From 1st August to 31st August 1916

Vol. 4.

61st Div. Sanitary Section
August 1916

Army Form C. 2118.

WAR DIARY
or
INTELLIGENCE SUMMARY. 61st D.S. Sanitary Section
(Erase heading not required.)

Place	Date	Hour	Summary of Events and Information	Remarks and references to Appendices
LA GORGUE	1/6/16		Routine Work	A.H.2
"	2/6/16		"	A.H.1
"	3/6/16		"	A.H.2
"	4/6/16		"	A.H.2
"	5/6/16		"	A.H.1
"	6/6/16		"	A.H.2
"	7/6/16		"	A.H.1
"	8/6/16		Water Cart consisting of 300 gallon tank fitted on G.S. Wagon employed for watering the streets of LA GORGUE, fitted with spraying apparatus	A.H.1
"	9/6/16		Routine Work	A.H.1
"	10/5/16		"	A.H.1
"	11/6/16		"	A.H.1
"	12/6/16		"	A.H.2
"	13/6/16		"	A.H.1
"	14/6/16		"	A.H.2

Army Form C. 2118.

WAR DIARY
or
INTELLIGENCE SUMMARY.
(Erase heading not required.)

Place	Date	Hour	Summary of Events and Information	Remarks and references to Appendices
LA GORGUE	15/9/16		Divisional Workshop opened under the Supervision of the SANITARY SECTION, for the manufacture of Sanitary Appliances for the Division such as:- Meat Safes, Portable Latrines, Grease Traps, Urinals, Ablution Benches etc. Four men from SANITARY SECTION working in the shop as follows:- Two Carpenters (including one Sergeant in charge) one plumber and one Sanitary engineer. One Carpenter attached to this "Unit" for duty in the Workshop from each Infantry Battalion in the Division and one hussar from the 182nd Inf. Bde. and from the 164th Inf. Bde. respectively.	(STH)
"	16/9/16		Routine Work	(STH)
"	17/9/16		"	(STH)
"	18/9/16		"	(STH)
"	19/9/16		Establishment of 23 "T.U." men attached to "Unit" for purpose of assisting with SANITARY WORK such as Town Sanitation, construction of incinerators, Camp Sanitation etc.	
"	"		20 men employed at Div Baths Laundry attached this "Unit" for Rick & Ration. 5 men employed at Div Drawing School and 3 men at Div Canteen attached for Rations.	(STH)

WAR DIARY
INTELLIGENCE SUMMARY.

Army Form C. 2118.

Place	Date	Hour	Summary of Events and Information	Remarks and references to Appendices
LA GORGUE	20/9/14		Routine Work	
"	21/9/14		"	
"	22/9/14		Sanitary Courses commenced by O.C. Sanitary Section. Course A for QMS's and Senior NCO's. 15 men reporting each 3rd day. Course consisted of lectures and practical demonstrations in Camp Sanitation and construction of Sanitary appliances. Course B for men of Sanitary Squads. One man drawn from each Squad. Six men report for a course of six days. Men go into Div. Workshop and learn how to make Sanitary appliances such as Grease traps, Ablution benches, Urinals, Latrines and meat safes from materials at hand. Period of Course – 22nd August to 30th September.	
"	28/9/14		Inspection of all horselines in DIVISIONAL AREA commenced and instructions given regarding disposal of manure.	
"	29/9/14		Routine Work	
"	30/9/14		"	

Army Form C. 2118.

WAR DIARY
or
INTELLIGENCE SUMMARY.
(Erase heading not required.)

Instructions regarding War Diaries and Intelligence Summaries are contained in F. S. Regs., Part II. and the Staff Manual respectively. Title pages will be prepared in manuscript.

Place	Date	Hour	Summary of Events and Information	Remarks and references to Appendices
LA GORGUE	20/3/16		Routine Work	1571)
"	27/3/16		"	1571)
"	23/3/16		"	1571)
"	29/3/16		"	1571)
"	30/3/16		Rcd DG from IIIrd Army of 3/16. All Officers' Messes in LA GORGUE and LAVENTIE inspected and reported on	1571) 1571)
"	31/3/16		During the month, the following Sanitary appliances were constructed and handed over to Units :— 6 Incinerators, 75 Portable latrines, 16 Grease traps, 11 Urinals, 5 Refuse bins, 9 Incinerator lids, 9 Ablution benches.	1571)

W.H. Davson Capt RAMC
OC. 61st Div Sanitary Section

Vol 5

Confidential.

War Diary
of
61st Divisional Sanitary Section

From 1st Sept. 1916   To. 30th Sept 1916

Volume 5.

COMMITTEE FOR THE
MEDICAL HISTORY OF THE WAR
Date   26 OCT.1916

Sept. 1916

Army Form C. 2118.

WAR DIARY
or
INTELLIGENCE SUMMARY.
(Erase heading not required.)

Instructions regarding War Diaries and Intelligence Summaries are contained in F.S. Regs., Part II. and the Staff Manual respectively. Title pages will be prepared in manuscript.

Place	Date	Hour	Summary of Events and Information	Remarks and references to Appendices
LA GORGUE	1/9/16		Routine Work	15HD
"	2/9/16		"	15HD
"	3/9/16		"	15HD
"	4/9/16		"	15HD
"	5/9/16		"	15HD
"	6/9/16		"	15HD
"	7/9/16		"	15HD
"	8/9/16		"	15HD
"	9/9/16		"	15HD
"	10/9/16		"	15HD
"	11/9/16		"	15HD
"	12/9/16		A Cooker for Camps and billets designed by Sergeant T. SLIM of this Unit and found to produce very satisfactory results. Examined and approved by the AA & QMG, 61st Division, and decided to use ever Cookers of this pattern in the Camps and billets of the DIVISIONAL AREA under the supervision of this NCO.	15HD

WAR DIARY
or
INTELLIGENCE SUMMARY.
(Erase heading not required.)

Army Form C. 2118.

Instructions regarding War Diaries and Intelligence Summaries are contained in F. S. Regs., Part II. and the Staff Manual respectively. Title pages will be prepared in manuscript.

Place	Date	Hour	Summary of Events and Information	Remarks and references to Appendices
LA GORGUE	13/9/14		Routine Work	WD
"	14/9/14		"	WD
"	15/9/14		A.D.M.S. of 3rd Division, inspected the DIVISIONAL WORKSHOP and SANITARY SECTION BILLET to see various Sanitary Appliances being manufactured and in use.	WD
"	16/9/14		The D.M.S. of FIRST ARMY inspected the SANITARY SECTION Office, Billet, and DIVISIONAL WORKSHOP, and saw the various Sanitary appliances in course of manufacture and in use, also the Charts and records of INFECTIOUS DISEASES, and the registration of all Water Supply in the Divisional Area on Special Map prepared by the SANITARY SECTION.	WD
"	17/9/14		Census of all houses in LA GORGUE commenced, and particulars as to disposal of refuse and General Sanitation recorded.	WD
"	18/9/14		O.C. Sanitary Section of 30th Division visited DIVISIONAL WORKSHOP and BILLET and saw various Sanitary appliances in course of manufacture and in use.	WD
"	19/9/14		Routine Work	WD

WAR DIARY or INTELLIGENCE SUMMARY.

Army Form C. 2118.

Place	Date	Hour	Summary of Events and Information	Remarks and references to Appendices
LA GORGUE	20/9/16		Commanding Officer attended a Conference at D.M.S. Office, FIRST ARMY at which the D.M.S. and all O's C SANITARY SECTIONS in the FIRST ARMY were present. It was arranged that O's C Sanitary Sections should visit the 61st DIV. SANITARY SECTION Headquarters and the 61st DIV WORKSHOP to inspect the manufacture of Sanitary appliances and the Records of INFECTIOUS DISEASES and WATER SUPPLY with a view to the adoption of similar measures in other Divisions of the FIRST ARMY.	
			Completion of house census in LA GORGUE. Map of this area prepared, each house being enumerated, and houses occupied by British Troops being specially noted.	
"	21/9/16		Routine Work.	WD
"	22/9/16		O's C Sanitary Sections of 6th, 32nd, 40th, & 31st Divisions visited DIVISIONAL WORKSHOP and SANITARY SECTION Headquarters by instructions of the D.M.S. FIRST ARMY	WD
"	23/9/16		O's C Sanitary Sections of both, 9th, 34th & 63 Divisions visited this Unit as above	WD

WAR DIARY
or
INTELLIGENCE SUMMARY.
(Erase heading not required.)

Army Form C. 2118.

Place	Date	Hour	Summary of Events and Information	Remarks and references to Appendices
LA GORGUE	24/9/16		Routine Work	65/1D
"	25/9/16		"	65/1D
"	26/9/16		"	65/1D
"	27/9/16		"	65/1D
"	28/9/16		"	65/1D
"	29/9/16		"	65/1D
"	30/9/16		"	65/1D
			During the month the following Sanitary appliances were constructed and handed over to Units :- 11 Incinerators, 6 Special Cookers, 296 Portable Latrines, 20 Grease traps, 61 "Meat Safes", 3 Ablution Benches, 23 Ablution Bowls, 71 Refuse Bins, 15 Urinals, 31 Box Latrines.	

19/10
2/10

15th Division R A McGregor Capt. R.A.M.C.
O.C. 61st Division Sant.

Vol 6

War Diary

61st Divisional Sanitary Section

From Oct 1st to Oct 31st 1916

Volume No 6

Confidential

Army Form C. 2118.

WAR DIARY
or
INTELLIGENCE SUMMARY.
(Erase heading not required.)

Instructions regarding War Diaries and Intelligence Summaries are contained in F. S. Regs., Part II. and the Staff Manual respectively. Title pages will be prepared in manuscript.

Place	Date	Hour	Summary of Events and Information	Remarks and references to Appendices
LA GORGUE	1/10/16		AAYQMG 36th Division visited the DIVISIONAL WORKSHOP and SANITARY SECTION BILLET to see various Sanitary Appliances being manufactured, and in use. Routine Work	WJ H.
"	2/10/16		"	WJ H
"	3/10/16		"	WJ H
"	4/10/16		"	WJ H
"	5/10/16		"	WJ H
"	6/10/16		Lecture by O.C. on Sanitation at DIVISIONAL SCHOOL ADMS and O.C Sanitary Section, 5th Division, visited the DIVISIONAL WORKSHOP and SANITARY SECTION BILLET to see various Sanitary appliances being manufactured and in use.	WJ H
"	7/10/16		Routine Work	WJ H
"	8/10/16		"	WJ H
"	9/10/16		"	WJ H
"	10/10/16		"	WJ H
"	11/10/16		"	WJ H
"	12/10/16		"	WJ H
"	13/10/16		"	WJ H

Army Form C. 2118.

WAR DIARY
or
INTELLIGENCE SUMMARY.
(Erase heading not required.)

Instructions regarding War Diaries and Intelligence Summaries are contained in F. S. Regs., Part II. and the Staff Manual respectively. Title pages will be prepared in manuscript.

Place	Date	Hour	Summary of Events and Information	Remarks and references to Appendices
LA GORGUE	14/10/16		Routine Work	1914
"	15/10/16		" "	1915
"	16/10/16		" "	1916
"	17/10/16		" "	1915
"	18/10/16		Special Crate to be fitted on Watercarts for the Carriage of additional water in Petrol Tins, designed by Private E. LONGBOTTOM, No. 97 of this unit, approved by Divisional Conference at H. Qrs. Manufacture of same commenced in DIVISIONAL WORKSHOP with a view to fitting all Watercarts in the Division.	1916
"	19/10/16		Routine Work	1914
"	20/10/16		" "	1914
"	21/10/16		" "	1914
"	22/10/16		All Watercarts in the DIVISION fitted with Watertight box for Bleaching & Clarifying powder	1916
"	23/10/16		" "	1916
"	24/10/16		" "	1915
"	25/10/16		" "	1916

2353 Wt. W2544/1454 700,000 5/15 D. D. & L. A.D.S.S./Forms/C. 2118.

Army Form C. 2118.

WAR DIARY
or
INTELLIGENCE SUMMARY.
(Erase heading not required.)

Instructions regarding War Diaries and Intelligence Summaries are contained in F.S. Regs., Part II. and the Staff Manual respectively. Title pages will be prepared in manuscript.

Place	Date	Hour	Summary of Events and Information	Remarks and references to Appendices
LA GORGUE	26/10/16		Routine Work	10it
"	27/10/16		Handed over all Billets, Billet fittings and Fixtures to OC Sanitary Section 38th Division	10it
ST VENANT	28/10/16		Unit moved to ST VENANT	10it
"	29/10/16		Routine Work	10it
"	30/10/16		"	10it
"	31/10/16		Completion of fitting all Infantry Units and Machine Gun Companies in the DIVISION with special crate for the carriage of additional water in Petrol tins, on water carts. During the month the following Sanitary appliances were constructed and handed over to Units:- 2 Incinerators, 5 Special Cookers, 26 meat Safes, 137 Portable Latrines, 19 Box Latrines, 14 Urinals, 9 Grease traps, 109 Refuse bins, 13 Ablution benches, 62 washing troughs, 61 waterable boxes for watercarts, 34 Special Crates for carrying Petrol tins on watercarts, 5 trench stoves, 20 doors & lids for incinerators.	10it

W. Hoyler Major
for Capt RANCT
OC 61 st Div Sanitary Section

Confidential

Vol 7 WAR DIARY
of
61st Div. Sanitary Section

From 1st Nov 16   To 30th Nov 16

Volumes No. 7

Vol 1

Army Form C. 2118.

WAR DIARY
or
INTELLIGENCE SUMMARY.
(Erase heading not required.)

Instructions regarding War Diaries and Intelligence Summaries are contained in F. S. Regs., Part II. and the Staff Manual respectively. Title pages will be prepared in manuscript.

Place	Date	Hour	Summary of Events and Information	Remarks and references to Appendices
ST. VENANT	1/11/16		Routine Work	157AD
CHELERS	2/11/16		Unit moved to CHELERS	157AD
"	3/11/16		Routine Work	107AD
ROLLECOURT	4/11/16		Unit moved to ROLLECOURT	107AD
"	5/11/16		Routine Work	107AD
FROHEN LE GRAND	6/11/16		Unit moved to FROHEN LE GRAND	107AD
"	7/11/16		Routine Work	157AD
"	8/11/16		"	67AD
"	9/11/16		Bodies for Divl Headquarters started by Unit at FROHEN LE GRAND	157AD
"	10/11/16		Routine Work	157AD
"	11/11/16		"	107AD
"	12/11/16		"	157AD
"	13/11/16		"	107AD
"	14/11/16		"	107AD
BERNAVILLE	15/11/16		Unit moved to BERNAVILLE	107AD
CANAPLES	16/11/16		Unit moved to CANAPLES	107AD

Army Form C. 2118.

WAR DIARY
or
INTELLIGENCE SUMMARY.
(Erase heading not required.)

Instructions regarding War Diaries and Intelligence Summaries are contained in F. S. Regs., Part II. and the Staff Manual respectively. Title pages will be prepared in manuscript.

Place	Date	Hour	Summary of Events and Information	Remarks and references to Appendices
CONTAY	17/11/16		Unit moved to CONTAY	15742
"	18/11/16		Routine Work	15742
"	19/11/16		"	15742
"	20/11/16		O.C. proceeded with DIVISIONAL WORKSHOP to W9d7.3 (Sheet 57D) to prepare Camp there for DIV. H.Qrs	15742
"	21/11/16		O.C. took charge of Water Supplies in new Divisional area from 19th Division	15722
W9d7.3 (Sheet 57D)	22/11/16		Remainder of Unit moved to W9d7.3 (Sheet 57D)	15722
	23/11/16		Pte. Duffield Rooms at the QUARRY, CRUCIFIX CORNER, W11d.1 (Sheet 57D) Arrangements made for the holding of all Water Supplies in the DIVISIONAL AREA as follows. CRUCIFIX CORNER Group with 1 NCO of SANITARY SECTION and 14 men distributed as follows:— CRUCIFIX CORNER STATION W11d 3. 3 men OVILLERS POST (tanks) W14 b1.7 and OVILLERS POST (taps) W14 b3.6. 1 man OVILLERS Group with 1 NCO of SANITARY SECTION and 3 men as follows:— OVILLERS ROAD X 6 c 3.5. 1 man. HUN TANK X 3 c1.9 and BENNETT STREET X 8 c 1.5. 1 man. DONNET POST X 7 c central and SECTION TANK X 7 d 7.3. 1 man. THIEPVAL ROAD Group with 1 NCO of SANITARY SECTION and 2 men as follows:— THIEPVAL ROAD R 32 b 6.4	15777

Army Form C. 2118.

WAR DIARY
or
INTELLIGENCE SUMMARY.
(Erase heading not required.)

Instructions regarding War Diaries and Intelligence Summaries are contained in F. S. Regs., Part II. and the Staff Manual respectively. Title pages will be prepared in manuscript.

Place	Date	Hour	Summary of Events and Information	Remarks and references to Appendices
W16 b.9.2 Sheet 57D	28/11/16		1 man, TAP SUPPLY R 32 c 6.8. 1 man, AUTHUILLE WOOD Group with 1 NCO of SANITARY SECTION and 2 men as follows:- TANKS X1d 9.9. 1 man, 2 TAPS X7 9 a central and WOOD POST X1c 6.4. 1 man, Sheet for map references 57D.	15TP
"	28/11/16		Routine Work	15TP
"	28/11/16		"	15TP
"	28/11/16		Water Supplies of OVILLERS Group and at OVILLERS POST (Maps) W16 b.1.7 and OVILLERS POST (Maps) W16 b.3.6 of CRUCIFIX CORNER Group handed over to the 51st DIVISION.	15TP
"	28/11/16		Routine Work	15TP
"	28/11/16		11 men attached to the SANITARY SECTION for work at Div Drying Rooms, billeted and rationed by this Unit Authority, 61st Division No A 466 of 29/11/16.	15TP
"	29/11/16		1 NCO of SANITARY SECTION and 4 men took over the Sanitation of MARTINSART.	15TP
"	30/11/16		Routine Work	16TP

W H Davison Capt RAMC
O/C 61st Div Sanitary Section

Confidential

War Diary

of

61st Divisional Sanitary Section

From 1st December 16   To 31st December 16

Volume No. 9

WAR DIARY
INTELLIGENCE SUMMARY

Vol. No 4

Army Form C. 2118.

Place	Date	Hour	Summary of Events and Information	Remarks and references to Appendices
W¹ⁿ⁷.2 Bray sur S	1/10/16		Routine Work	appx D
"	2/10/16		A complete survey of the Sanitary Conditions of MARTINSART, W3 sheet 57d completed, records calculated and recorded on map scale 1/2,500, and steps taken for arrangements made in conjunction with Town Major to improve the existing conditions.	appx D
"	3/10/16		Routine Work	appx D
"	4/10/16		" "	appx D
"	5/10/16		" "	appx D
"	6/10/16		" "	appx D
"	7/10/16		" "	appx D
"	8/10/16		" "	appx D
"	9/10/16		" "	appx D
"	10/10/16		" "	appx D
"	11/10/16		" "	appx D
"	12/10/16		" "	appx D
"	13/10/16		" "	appx D

WAR DIARY
or
INTELLIGENCE SUMMARY.
(Erase heading not required.)

Army Form C. 2118.

Instructions regarding War Diaries and Intelligence Summaries are contained in F. S. Regs., Part II. and the Staff Manual respectively. Title pages will be prepared in manuscript.

Place	Date	Hour	Summary of Events and Information	Remarks and references to Appendices
W.1 E.7.2 Sheet 5 1/8	14/12/14		Routine Work	1617
"	15/12/14		"	1617
"	16/12/14		"	1617
"	17/12/14		"	1617
"	18/12/14		"	1617
"	19/12/14		"	1617
"	20/12/14		"	1617
"	21/12/14		"	1617
"	22/12/14		"	1617
"	23/12/14		Completion of Map of the forward half of DIVISIONAL AREA, Scale 1/5000, showing the pumping stations and points at which water can be obtained, also the Sanitary arrangements of all camps and billets.	1617
"	24/12/14		Routine Work	1617
"	25/12/14		"	1617
"	26/12/14		A monthly Sanitary report was furnished showing the incidence of disease in the Division for the month. The report also included a record of the steps taken during the	1617

WAR DIARY
or
INTELLIGENCE SUMMARY.
(Erase heading not required.)

Army Form C. 2118.

Place	Date	Hour	Summary of Events and Information	Remarks and references to Appendices
			month to improve the Sanitation of the Divisional area, particularly the village of MARTINSART, W3, sheet 57d, which was taken over in a very insanitary condition.	65AD
W47.3	24/9/16		A survey of the Sanitary conditions of HEDAUVILLE, P34 sheet 57d in detail was commenced, similar to that done in the case of MARTINSART. All water supplies dumps in the forward half of Divisional Area labelled, and an office record made to shew the details and arrangements of all these water supplies.	65AD
"	28/9/16		Routine Work	65AD
"	29/9/16		"	65AD
"	30/9/16		"	65AD
"	31/9/16		"	65AD
			During the month the following Sanitary appliances were constructed and handed over to Units :- 2 Incinerators, 1 large enough to deal with all the refuse of MARTINSART W3 sheet 57d, 2 Special Cookers, 10 Portable Latrines, 10 Box Latrines of one to six seats supplied and fixed into position	

WAR DIARY
or
INTELLIGENCE SUMMARY.
(Erase heading not required.)

Army Form C. 2118.

Place	Date	Hour	Summary of Events and Information	Remarks and references to Appendices
			With frame round Corrugated iron roof, and canvas sides. "Public Urinal, NUMBER ONE 115 Urinals, 6 Stoves with piping, and a large quantity of notice boards.	WAP
			B.H. Dawson Cpl. RAMC
o/c 161st Div Sanitary Section	

Vol 10

Confidential

War Diary

of

61st Div. Sanitary Section

From 1/3/17 to 31/3/17

Volume No. 10

WAR DIARY
or
INTELLIGENCE SUMMARY.
(Erase heading not required.)

Army Form C. 2118.

Vol. No. 10

Place	Date	Hour	Summary of Events and Information	Remarks and references to Appendices
W¹⁰⁸⁹.2 Sheet 5⁷ᵈ.3	1/2/19		Instructions received to rejoin the 61st Division as per the following extract from W.E. from 2nd Corps No. Z1991 of 1/2/19 "The 5th Army also being the following moves of Sanitary Sections will take place forthwith W51st Divnl Sanitary Section will rejoin their Division under divisional arrangements leaving their present area on 10th inst	(5HD)
"	3/2/19		Routine Work	(SHD)
"	3/2/19		"	(SHD)
"	4/2/19		"	(SHD)
"	5/2/19		Handed over to 35th Sanitary Section 16th Division on relief. Particulars of Water Supplies in 16th Divisional AREA, Accounts of infectious diseases in 16th Division, Map of MARTINSART W3 sheet 57d, HEDAUVILLE P34 sheet 57d, and VARENNES P25 & 31 Sheet 57d Scale 1/2500 shewing positions of Water points, Latrines and incinerators, also map of the 16th Divisional AREA Scale 1/5000 with similar particulars	(5HD)
"			Unit together with Workshop personnel and other 61st Divisional personnel attached moved from W¹⁰⁸⁹.2 Sheet 5⁷ᵈ to LONG near ABBEVILLE and rejoined the 61st Division	
LONG	6/2/19			(5HD)

Army Form C. 2118.

WAR DIARY
or
INTELLIGENCE SUMMARY.
(Erase heading not required.)

Instructions regarding War Diaries and Intelligence Summaries are contained in F. S. Regs., Part II. and the Staff Manual respectively. Title pages will be prepared in manuscript.

Place	Date	Hour	Summary of Events and Information	Remarks and references to Appendices
LONG	7/2/17		The following villages visited and a systematic inspection made of Sanitary conditions :- AILLY-LE-HAUT-CLOCHER, FONTAINE-sur-SOMME, LONGPRE, BRAY, YAUCOURT, BELLANCOURT, LIERCOURT, L'ÉTOILE, VILLERS-sous-AILLY, BRUCHAMPS, GORENFLOS, ERGNIES, BUIGNY L'ABBÉ, BUSSUS-BUSSUE. Steps taken to get all incinerators in the AREA working. Various water points visited, the water tested, and units notified where good water could be obtained.	15HD
"	8/2/17		Systematic inspection of all Divisional Water Carts commenced. A considerable number of these were out of use owing to the very severe frost. Repairs effected at Ordnance Workshop ABBÉVILLE.	15HD
"	9/2/17		Routine Work	15HD
"	10/2/17		" "	15HD
"	11/2/17		" "	15HD
"	12/2/17		The Thresh disinfector, which had been removed from this Unit to accompany the 61st Division on move of 16/1/17 re-attached to Unit for working arrangements and fuel supplies.	15HD
"	13/2/17		Routine Work	15HD

Army Form C. 2118.

WAR DIARY
or
INTELLIGENCE SUMMARY.
(Erase heading not required.)

Instructions regarding War Diaries and Intelligence Summaries are contained in F. S. Regs., Part II. and the Staff Manual respectively. Title pages will be prepared in manuscript.

Place	Date	Hour	Summary of Events and Information	Remarks and references to Appendices
GUILLAUCOURT	14/9/19		Unit moved from LONG to GUILLAUCOURT W.14. Rosières combined sheet.	(STD)
"	15/9/19		A Survey of the Sanitary conditions, in detail, of GUILLAUCOURT W.14. commenced. Routine work.	(STD)
"	16/9/19			(STD)
"	17/9/19		House to house Survey of GUILLAUCOURT completed, the water points tested and labelled re chlorination, all other wells in the village labelled "Not to be used for troops" and map scale 1/2500 prepared shewing position of all billets and water points. Sanitary conditions recorded and tabulated. A Survey of the Sanitary conditions, in detail of FRAMERVILLE, R.29.3 and RAINECOURT R.33.y.34. Rosières combined sheet commenced. O.C. interviewed Officer of Trench Water Service.	(STD) (STD)
HARBONNIÈRES	18/9/19		Unit moved from GUILLAUCOURT W.14. to HARBONNIÈRES W.11.	(STD)
"	19/9/19		House to house Survey of FRAMERVILLE R.29.3 and RAINECOURT R.33.y.34. completed, Water points tested and labelled, and all records tabulated. A Survey of the Sanitary conditions, in detail of HARBONNIÈRES W.11. commenced.	(STD)
"	20/9/19		O.C. visited the forward area with Officer of Trench Water Service, and noted the position and condition of all wells which supply the TRENCHES and FORWARD AREA	(STD)

Army Form C. 2118.

WAR DIARY
or
INTELLIGENCE SUMMARY.
(Erase heading not required.)

Place	Date	Hour	Summary of Events and Information	Remarks and references to Appendices
HARBONNIERES	21/9/17		Map prepared of RAINECOURT, R33&34, scale 1/2500, shewing position of all billets and water points.	(SPD)
"	22/9/17		House to house survey of HARBONNIERES, W11, completed, water points tested and labelled, and all records tabulated. A survey of the Sanitary conditions in detail, of VAUVILLERS, X6 Rosières commenced sheet commenced. Instructions received and complied with from 1st Division, letter number Q690 of 21/9/17 to select a man from the Sanitary Section to down majors of each of the following places:- MARCELCAVE, V9&10, HARBONNIERES W11, VAUVILLERS X6, FRAMERVILLE, R2&3, GUILLAUCOURT W14, and WIENCOURT V12 W7, to act as Sanitary expert. (Rosières continued sheet)	
"	23/9/17		Routine Work	(SPD)
"	24/9/17		House to house survey of VAUVILLERS, X6 completed, water points tested and labelled, and all records tabulated. Sanitary report for period 21/9/17 to 23/9/17 sent to ADMS	(SPD)
"	25/9/17		Map of FRAMERVILLE, R2&3, scale 1/2500 prepared shewing position of all billets and water points.	(SPD)
"	26/9/17		OC attended conference at D.D.M.S. office, 4th Corps	(SPD)

WAR DIARY
or
INTELLIGENCE SUMMARY.

Army Form C. 2118.

Place	Date	Hour	Summary of Events and Information	Remarks and references to Appendices
HARBONNIERES	24/2/17		Map of VAUVILLERS X 6, scale 1/2500 prepared shewing position of all billets and water points. House to house survey of WIENCOURT, V13 & W1, water points tested and labelled, and all records tabulated. Map, scale 1/2500 prepared shewing position of all billets and water points. Instructions received from 61st Division, concentration of letter number Q.690 of 21/2/17 that Town Majors will indent on O.C. Divisional Sanitary Section for latrine seats, screens etc and select sites for latrines and watering places in conjunction with him. Steps taken to procure the necessary materials.	15H.D 15H.D
"	28/2/17		Routine work. During the month the following Sanitary appliances were constructed and handed over to units:- 2 Incinerators, 2 special cookers, 112 portable latrines, 19 box latrines of one to ten seats, and 10 urinals, and a large number of notices. During the month the 61st Division was transferred from the 5th Army to the 4th Army and in consequence 5th Army Routine Order No 263 of 9/1/9/16 making Sanitary Sections Army Troops, and in so far doing removing them from the Divisions was rendered inoperative. In consequence when the Sanitary Section rejoined the Division on 6/2/17 the Section again came under divisional arrangements	

WAR DIARY or INTELLIGENCE SUMMARY

Army Form C. 2118.

Place	Date	Hour	Summary of Events and Information	Remarks and references to Appendices
			and the objections set out in the WAR DIARY for January 1917 ceased to exist from that date. The Headquarters Staff of the Division, who had made every effort to retain the Section in the Division, expressed satisfaction at the return, at the time, to the Division, and the working arrangements which had existed prior to January 16th 1917 were resumed. Records of infectious diseases occurring in this Division during the three weeks that the Section was attached to the 18th Division, were handed over, and a continuous record has thus been kept.

The sanitation of the present area taken over from the French on 14/2/17 is very bad. The latrine accommodation in all the villages was found to be very insufficient, resulting in very extensive fouling of the ground surrounding billets, which must have existed for a very considerable time. The Section, in conjunction with the Workshop, is making every effort to deal with this state of affairs, and without such a Workshop the task of putting an area like this in a reasonable sanitary condition, and to treat all water founds, positions of incinerators, latrines etc. would not seem to be possible within a reasonable time. The question of supply of material, which is always a difficulty. One installation by the Construction of sanitary appliances by a Divisional area has been solved by an arrangement that (1) The S.S.O. of the Division grants permission to draw a certain proportion of biscuit boxes, bacon boxes and other ration boxes, and (2) Inf. of 1st Division letter No. Q590 of 30/2/17 granting authority to draw the necessary materials from the Divisional R.E.s. The Section is therefore able, not only to construct sanitary appliances but to supply material to Town Majors and Divisional Unit when it is found necessary to augment the issue of such appliances made from the Sanitary Section Workshop. | |

F.H. Dosser Capt RAMC
O/C 61st Div Sanitary Section

Not Secret

Vol XI

140/2043

WAR DIARY
of
61st Div Sanitary Section

from 1st March 1917 to 31st March 1917

Volume number 11

COMMITTEE FOR THE
MEDICAL HISTORY OF THE WAR
Date 11 MAY 1917

Vol 11

Army Form C. 2118.

WAR DIARY
or
INTELLIGENCE SUMMARY.

(Erase heading not required.)

Instructions regarding War Diaries and Intelligence Summaries are contained in F. S. Regs., Part II. and the Staff Manual respectively. Title pages will be prepared in manuscript.

Place	Date	Hour	Summary of Events and Information	Remarks and references to Appendices
HARBONNIERES	1/3/17		Routine Work	6547
"	2/3/17		"	6547
"	3/3/17		"	6547
"	4/3/17		"	6547
"	5/3/17		"	6547
"	6/3/17		"	6547
"	7/3/17		"	6547
"	8/3/17		"	6547
"	9/3/17		"	6547
"	10/3/17		"	6547
"	11/3/17		"	6547
"	12/3/17		O.C. visited the Sanitary Officer of the 16th Division and was shown over a "Javelising" plant at CAPPY.	6547
"	13/3/17		Routine Work	6547
"	14/3/17		"	6547

WAR DIARY
or
INTELLIGENCE SUMMARY.
(Erase heading not required.)

Army Form C. 2118.

Place	Date	Hour	Summary of Events and Information	Remarks and references to Appendices
HARBONNIERS	15/3/17		Inspection by ADMS who visited the Sanitary Section Office and Workshop, and saw charts and records of INFECTIOUS DISEASE, models of sanitary appliances, and the various appliances in course of construction.	(SA)
"	16/3/17		Routine Work	(SA)
"	17/3/17		" "	(SA)
"	18/3/17		" "	(SA)
"	19/3/17		Five men of the Sanitary Section, accompanied by five men of the Workshop proceeded to CHAULNES, A & S Rogures continued sheet. A general survey of the town was made with a view of discovering suitable water supplies, and putting them in working order. From this point the men proceeded to forward villages as the advance continued. All wells in CHAULNES except one, situated at the Chateau, were found to have been destroyed either by shell fire or by troops. Many of the wells appear to have been blown up intentionally and rubbish thrown into them so as to render them useless. One of the chief water supplies, a horse propelled pump, appeared to have been smashed intentionally, and the well partly filled up. The town was in ruins, and with the exception of a few dugouts and cellars, there was no accommodation	(SA)

2353 Wt. W2514/1454 700,000 5/15 D. D. & L. A.D.S.S./Forms/C. 2118.

WAR DIARY
or
INTELLIGENCE SUMMARY.
(Erase heading not required.)

Place	Date	Hour	Summary of Events and Information	Remarks and references to Appendices
			for troops. Practically every house and space in the town was fouled with excreta. The village OMIECOURT was visited, and one well was found fit. All other wells in this village which was in ruins were polluted to such an extent as to render them useless (map ref. B.6. Rosieres combined sheet)	AFD
HARBONNIERES	20/3/19		The following villages were visited by men of the Sanitary Section with a view to surveying and testing water supplies and labelling those found fit for drinking. All these villages were found to be in ruins, and in some instances were burning at the time of visit:— MARCELPOT, T.22 & 26, Rosieres combined sheet, one well was discovered fit, and in working order. LICOURT T.30 & B.6, Rosieres combined sheet. One well was discovered fit and in working order. All other wells were polluted. PARGNY, C.10 Rosieres combined sheet, 20 wells were discovered, but owing to damaged pumps and filling in with rubbish water could be obtained from 5 only. One of these was badly polluted with manure, and the other 4 gave water fit for drinking. The SOMME River and Canal were also tested at this point; the water from the Canal appeared slightly cloudy, but samples from both sources shewed only one measure	AFD

WAR DIARY
or
INTELLIGENCE SUMMARY.
(Erase heading not required.)

Army Form C. 2118.

Place	Date	Hour	Summary of Events and Information	Remarks and references to Appendices
			of bleaching powder necessary to sterilize. BETHENCOURT, B31 Rogieres contained sheet, one principal supply, a large chain draw well was in working order, also pump apparently supplied from Somme Canal. The ruins of this village were burning at time of survey. MORCHAIN C 13 & 14 Rogieres contained sheet. There was no water in this village fit for drinking. The wells that were accessable appear to have been used as latrines. FONTAINE LE PARGNY, all wells were found to have been destroyed.	(SP)
HARBONNIERES	21/3/17		ÉPENANCOURT, C3, Rogieres contained sheet. A Spring was discovered at the Sugar Factory with excellent water and living fish, covered but fallen brickwork. Site cleared and made accessable to water carts.	(SP)
"	22/3/17		DRESLINCOURT B 24 & 29, Rogieres contained sheet. One well discovered with good water and in working order. All other wells destroyed. BERSAUCOURT, B31 Rogieres contained sheet. All wells found to have been destroyed. POTTE, B24, Rogieres contained sheet, only one supply in this village, but not in working order. All other wells destroyed.	(SP)

Army Form C. 2118.

WAR DIARY
or
INTELLIGENCE SUMMARY.
(Erase heading not required.)

Instructions regarding War Diaries and Intelligence Summaries are contained in F.S. Regs., Part II. and the Staff Manual respectively. Title pages will be prepared in manuscript.

Place	Date	Hour	Summary of Events and Information	Remarks and references to Appendices
HARBONNIERES	22/3/1"		Baths:- A local Brewery at HARBONNIERES was altered so as to arrange for the bathing of 1000 men per day, including treatment for trench feet and the ironing of verminous clothing. This work was carried out by the Sanitary Section Workshop and completed on the 23rd.	(WD)
"	23/3/1"		The Sanitary Officer of the British Expeditionary Forces in FRANCE, accompanied by the Sanitary Officer of the Fourth Army, visited this unit for the purpose of viewing models of sanitary appliances which have been adopted by this Section for use in the field, with success. He also inspected the Sanitary Section Workshop, as well as the general work of the Unit, including records & charts of all Infectious Disease in the 51st Division during its service in FRANCE, and took with him samples of the maps demonstrating the position of water supplies and particulars of sanitation in the various villages. On leaving, he expressed his appreciation of everything he had seen and of the work of the Unit generally, and requested that working drawings of the sanitary appliances in use be sent to him at a favourable opportunity.	(SH)

T2134. Wt. W708—776. 50C000. 4/15. Sir J. C. & S.

Army Form C. 2118.

WAR DIARY
or
INTELLIGENCE SUMMARY.
(Erase heading not required.)

Place	Date	Hour	Summary of Events and Information	Remarks and references to Appendices
HARBONNIERES	23/3/17		OC proceeded to PERTAIN, B10 Rogières continued sheet, and CROIX MOLIGNAUX D69.9 sheet 62c SW, billeting at PERTAIN for the night, and arranged for the inspection of Water Supplies East of the SOMME and 7 men of the Unit billeted at CROIX MOLIGNAUX to carry out water duties from that point, this arrangement being necessary owing to the fact that Divisional Headquarters was still at HARBONNIERES.	
			The village of VILLECOURT C24 Rogières continued sheet was visited, and it was found that all wells had been filled with manure and rubbish, the only available water supply being the River SOMME nearby.	(Std)
	24/3/17		The following villages were visited by men of the Sanitary Section with a view to surveying and testing water supplies and labelling those found fit for drinking. All these villages were found to be in ruins.	
			FALVY, C5 Rogières continued sheet. A spring and one well were discovered in this village, and both supplies gave good water. Y, D15 & 19 sheet 62c SW; only one well exists in this village with good water. All other wells filled with manure and debris. MONCHY LAGACHE V.R.18 sheet 62c SW, eight wells	(Std)

T2134. Wt. W708—776. 50,000. 4/15. Sir J. C. & S.

Army Form C. 2118.

WAR DIARY
or
INTELLIGENCE SUMMARY.
(Erase heading not required.)

Instructions regarding War Diaries and Intelligence Summaries are contained in F.S. Regs., Part II. and the Staff Manual respectively. Title pages will be prepared in manuscript.

Place	Date	Hour	Summary of Events and Information	Remarks and references to Appendices
			were discovered in this village. Spring food water and in working order. CROIX MOLIGNAUX D 6.9.9, sheet 62cS.W.; only one foot supply was found in this village. Windlass repaired and buckets fitted by Sanitary Section. Nearly every house in this village has a draw well, but these have all been filled with debris.	(SH)
HARBONNIERES	26/3/17		MOLIGNAUX, D.3, sheet 62cS.W.; One well was found in good order & giving food water. All other wells filled with manure and debris. FLEZ, V.23, sheet 62cS.W., all wells in this village were found to have been so contaminated as to be useless. DOUVIEUX, V.23, sheet 62cS.W.; only one usable well found in this village. GUIZANCOURT, V.26, sheet 62cS.W.; only one usable well in this village.	(SH)
"	26/3/17		MONTECOURT, V.11, sheet 62cS.W.; only one well in working order was found in this village. MERAUCOURT, V.6&12, sheet 62cS.W.; Six shallow wells were discovered and all have good water.	(SH)
"	27/3/17		ATHIES, U.12 & V.7, sheet 62cS.W.; four good wells were discovered but only one was in working order. An excellent spring was also found in the hillside west of the village at V.13.b.6.8. FORQUES, V.13, sheet 62cS.W., no wells were left in this village in a condition to be used or easily made so, but the River OMIGNON	(SH)

Army Form C. 2118.

WAR DIARY
or
INTELLIGENCE SUMMARY.
(Erase heading not required.)

Place	Date	Hour	Summary of Events and Information	Remarks and references to Appendices
			at V7 d 0.3 was tested and gave good results. ENNEMAIN, V17 16, Rogeries combined sheet; all wells had been rendered useless. A spring at V19 b 7 and the stream at V19 b7.4 were tested and gave good results. TERRY, W2, sheet 62cSW; eight wells in this village gave bad water. CAULAINCOURT, W4 9.5, sheet 62c SW; all wells in this village so polluted as to be useless. but the River OMIGNON on the outskirts of the village and three springs nearby. Give good water. TREFCON, W10, sheet 62c SW; all wells in this village rendered quite useless. Routine Work.	65475
HARBONNIERES	28/3/19			15745
CROIX MOLIGNAUX	29/3/19		The Unit under orders from A.D.M.S. moved from HARBONNIERES to CROIX MOLIGNAUX, and great difficulty was experienced in moving stores and transport owing to the unsatisfactory condition of the roads. When Unit arrived at CROIX MOLIGNAUX, the place was found in ruins, and no billets were available. The Section proceeded to erect office and billets and this was completed on the 31st. The village of Villers-Eve VILLÉVEQUE, W12 9 x 7, sheet 62c SW, was visited re water supply, and all wells were found to have been rendered useless. The River	15745

Army Form C. 2118.

WAR DIARY
or
INTELLIGENCE SUMMARY.
(Erase heading not required.)

Place	Date	Hour	Summary of Events and Information	Remarks and references to Appendices
			OMIGNON passing this village was tested, and shewed two measures of Bleaching powder necessary to sterilize.	A/STP
CROIX MOLIGNAUX	30/3/17		Routine Work	A/STP
"	31/3/17		" "	6/STP
			During the month the following sanitary appliances were constructed and handed over to units:- 5 incinerators, 1 special large meat safe, 65 portable latrines, 15 box latrines of one seat, 13 box latrines of two to nine seats with framework and screening complete, 12 public urinals, and 2 pedestal urinals. Also, over 400 notices and signboards were made and painted. The sanitary arrangements of villages near the German lines were found to be in an unsatisfactory condition, but the villages near the River SOMME and east of the SOMME appear to have been good. All latrines were burnt by the enemy. There is also evidence of elaborate bathing facilities in several of the villages.	6/STP

W H Davison Capt
O.C. 61St Div. Sanitary Section

T2134. Wt. W708—776. 500000. 4/15. Sir J. C. & S.

Confidential
Vol 12

War Diary

of

61st Div. Sanitary Section

for April 1917

Volume No. 12

Volume No. 12

WAR DIARY
or
INTELLIGENCE SUMMARY.

Army Form C. 2118.

Place	Date	Hour	Summary of Events and Information	Remarks and references to Appendices
CROIX MOLIGNAUX D46g Sheet 62cSW	1/4/17		Routine Work	WD
"	2/4/17		The following places were visited by men of the Sanitary Section with a view to inspecting and testing water supplies, and those found fit for drinking were labelled accordingly:- SOYECOURT R16d., MARTEVILLE R22d.	WD
"	3/4/17		VERMAND R21&32, BEAUVOIS W22&23, POEUILLY Q26&29, BIHECOURT R15&22, VILLECHOLLES R21 and ATTILLY X 9 & 10 sheet 62c SW.	WD
"	4/4/17		Routine Work	WD
"	5/4/17		"	WD
"	6/4/17		"	WD
"	7/4/17		"	WD
"	8/4/17		"	WD
"	9/4/17		"	WD
"	10/4/17		"	WD

Army Form C. 2118.

WAR DIARY
or
INTELLIGENCE SUMMARY.
(Erase heading not required.)

Place	Date	Hour	Summary of Events and Information	Remarks and references to Appendices
CROIX MOLIGNAUX	11/4/17		The O.C. proceeded to South Army Headquarters to carry out the duties of DADMS (Sanitation) during that Officer's absence on leave, and Captain W.G. Hirst, of 2/1st South Midland Field Ambulance arrived to act as O.C. of the Unit for that period.	137?
"	12/4/17		The 61st Division moved from this area, the 35th Division taking over from them. This Unit remained at CROIX MOLIGNAUX by orders of the ADMS.	W9H
"	13/4/17		Routine Work	W9H
"	14/4/17		"	W9H
"	15/4/17		"	W9H
"	16/4/17		"	W9H
"	17/4/17		"	W9H
"	18/4/17		Instructions received from IV Corps number 1660 A of 13/4/17 that Sanitary Sections be withdrawn from their divisions and constituted as Army troops, in accordance with G.H.Q. letter number DG/D/2366/15 "A" of 13/3/17, and a map was furnished defining the Sanitary area to be supervised by this Section. It extended from the River SOMME to the front line, and included about 25 villages. This area was occupied by troops of three divisions, namely:- the 35th, the 32nd	W9H

WAR DIARY
or
INTELLIGENCE SUMMARY.

(Erase heading not required.)

Army Form C. 2118.

Place	Date	Hour	Summary of Events and Information	Remarks and references to Appendices
CROIX MOLIGNAUX			and the 5th Cavalry Division, and certain other formations, such as:- the 6th RNAS, 2nd RFC, and the DAC and Artillery Brigades of the 61st Division.	
"	19/4/17		MAISSEMY R.19.23 sheet 62cSW was visited by OC re Sanitation and Water supplies. Routine Work	15/H 20/H
"	20/4/17			
"	21/4/17		A detachment from this unit proceed to TERRY W.2, sheet 62cSW. to establish billets there, from which the advanced half of this Sanitary Area can be conveniently worked. Routine Work	15/H 60/H 65/H 69/H
"	22/4/17		"	
"	23/4/17		"	
"	24/4/17		O.C. returned to Unit from Fourth Army Headquarters for duty, and Capt. AD Moist the acting O.C. returned to the 3/1st South Mid Field Ambulance. Visit of OC Sanitary Section of 5th Cavalry Division, who saw models and working drawings of sanitary appliances, and the various appliances in course of construction. The various questions dealing with sanitary matters were discussed, and an arrangement was made that 2 of his NCOs should visit this Workshop, and become familiar with the sanitary structures and methods which were decided to be suitable for the Area.	SHD
"	26/4/17			

WAR DIARY
or
INTELLIGENCE SUMMARY.
(Erase heading not required.)

Army Form C. 2118.

Place	Date	Hour	Summary of Events and Information	Remarks and references to Appendices
CROIX MOLIGNAUX	26/11/17		Arrangements made for the daily inspection and sanitary control, by men of this Unit, of the following towns and villages:- DEVISE V9a, MONTECOURT V6&12, MERAUCOURT V6&12 sheet 62c S.W. FALVY C5, ENNEMAIN U14&16, Rouières Combinedsheet, MARTEVILLE R32d, VILLEVEQUE W13&7, MONCHY LAGACHE V13&16, FLEZ V23, DOUVIEUX V23, GUIZANCOURT V26, MOLIGNAUX D3, VERMAND R26&32, TREFCON W10, TERRY W2, ATHIES U1&V7, FOURQUES V13, CAULAINCOURT W4&5, POEUILLY Q24&29, SOVECOURT R16d, Y D13&19, and CROIX MOLIGNAUX D7&9, sheet 62c S.W. D.C. visited A.D.M.S. 36th 61st Division re sanitation of the part of this sanitary area occupied by troops of that Division, and made satisfactory working arrangements re same.	137?
"	27/11/17		In accordance with instructions received from 61st Division, all men attached to this Unit were returned to 61st D.S.H.Qrs. Seventy four men were returned, fourteen forming the attached personnel of Sanitary section Workshop, and then being sanitary fatigues. The tools used by these fourteen men in the Workshop were also returned to the 61st Division. The Medical Officers of the 10th RNAS and 24th R.F.C. visited this Unit and O.C. gave a demonstration, by means of models and working drawings, of all	

WAR DIARY
or
INTELLIGENCE SUMMARY.
(Erase heading not required.)

Army Form C. 2118.

Place	Date	Hour	Summary of Events and Information	Remarks and references to Appendices
CROIX MOLIGNAUX			Sanitary appliances in use by this Section. W. expressed a wish to take copies of these drawings in order to construct similar appliances, and sent 2 men for this purpose.	SAP
"	28/4/17		O.C. together with A.D.M.S. 35th Division, visited, for purpose of inspection of sanitary conditions, various billeting areas occupied by units of the 35th, 32nd, 61st and 5th Cavalry Divisions. Instructions were given to these units re provision of proper latrines, disposal of bath effluent, disposal of manure, storage of food, and such other points that were noted.	SAP
"	29/4/17		Visit of two Officers of Sixth R.F.C. to inspect models and working drawings of sanitary appliances, and arrangements made for them to send a skilled Carpenter to this workshop for purpose of constructing similar appliances under the supervision of Sanitary Section N.C.O.	(SAP)
"	30/4/17		Visit of A.D.M.S. 5th Cavalry Division, when question of appointing Down wagons, disposal of manure, and method of disposal of baths effluent were discussed. Visit of three Medical Officers from 5th Cavalry Division and one from 32nd Division for purpose of inspecting models and working drawings of sanitary appliances in use by this Unit.	(SAP)

Army Form C. 2118.

WAR DIARY
or
INTELLIGENCE SUMMARY.
(Erase heading not required.)

Instructions regarding War Diaries and Intelligence Summaries are contained in F.S. Regs., Part II. and the Staff Manual respectively. Title pages will be prepared in manuscript.

Place	Date	Hour	Summary of Events and Information	Remarks and references to Appendices
CROIX MOLIGNAUX			During the month the following were constructed:- 3 Incinerators, 15 portable latrines, 16 box latrines of 6 seats, 3 of 8 seats, 1 of 4 seats, 1 of 3 seats, and 6 of 1 seat, 4 trough urinals, 1 special crate for carrying petrol tins or water cans. Also a German latrine was converted into a fly proof 10 seat latrine, and over 400 notices and sign boards were made and painted. Owing to the difficulty of obtaining labour due:- (1). To the fact that all fatigues attached to this Unit and supplied by the 61st Division had been withdrawn, and no fatigues to replace them had been supplied by the incoming Divisions. (2). No Town Majors had been appointed to any of the villages and billeting areas in the district, except that of MONCHY LAGACHE, only 4 of the 16 box latrines intended to be used as public latrines were placed in position. The question of the supply of fatigues, and the absence of Town Majors was made the subject of remarks in the "Sanitary Report" rendered to IV Corps, and correspondence is passing on the subject at present.	

A 5834 Wt. W4973/M687 750,000 8/16 D. D. & L. Ltd. Forms/C.2118/13.

WAR DIARY
or
INTELLIGENCE SUMMARY.
(Erase heading not required.)

Army Form C. 2118.

Place	Date	Hour	Summary of Events and Information	Remarks and references to Appendices
CROIX MOLIGNAUX			In volume number 9, some general remarks were made on the subject of the removal of Sanitary Sections from Divisions, and experience has again confirmed the opinion expressed in that volume. The difficulties experienced in dealing with several formations in the same area are very great. Each ADMS of a division has his own ideas and standards of what sanitary measures are required for his formation. Further villages and billeting areas are frequently occupied by troops of two or more divisions at the same time, and differences of opinion as to the standards of sanitation make it very difficult indeed for the N.C.O. of the Sanitary Section who is inspecting that district, to see that the scheme of sanitation recommended by this unit is carried out. Again, the question of obtaining fatigues under these circumstances for dealing with matters which pertain to the area more than to the individual unit is difficult, and considerable delay has already been experienced, although the ADsMS concerned have always been most anxious to help.

The removal of a number of skilled men who have worked with this unit for months, together with their tools, has completely disorganized the work of this unit. At present there is no authority for the acquisition of these tools, and in consequence all constructional work is at a standstill.

While this Sanitary Section remained with its Division no difficulties of this nature were experienced, the personal element, which is always an | |

Army Form C. 2118.

WAR DIARY
or
INTELLIGENCE SUMMARY.
(Erase heading not required.)

Place	Date	Hour	Summary of Events and Information	Remarks and references to Appendices
CROIX MOLIGNAUX			importance one in dealing with sanitary matters, was sufficient to overcome all difficulties. Under present arrangements, however, formal authority is required for everything, and more definite instructions, defining the duties and scope of a Sanitary Section are necessary.	

W.H. Dawson
Capt RAMC
O.C. 61st Div Sanitary Section

www.ingramcontent.com/pod-product-compliance
Lightning Source LLC
Chambersburg PA
CBHW081452160426
43193CB00013B/2456